Saving Ben

by Sandra Widener
illustrated by Erica Labarre

Orlando Boston Dallas Chicago San Diego

Visit *The Learning Site!*
www.harcourtschool.com

A woman walked along the beach one morning and saw something large and black on the sand. As she got closer, she saw that it was a young killer whale. This animal was in trouble.

Killer whales live in oceans. They need to be in water. If they are stranded on a beach, they can die quickly. When that woman in New Zealand saw the beached whale, she called for help.

One of the people who came was Ingrid Visser. She is a scientist who works for Project Jonah. Ingrid collects information about whales. Project Jonah works to save whales in New Zealand.

To Ingrid Visser, the young whale looked fine. She thought that maybe the whale had been chasing stingrays, which killer whales like to eat. "He probably just made a mistake chasing them in water that was too shallow," she said.

Killer whales can travel hundreds of miles in days.

The young whale was stuck on the beach. The rescuers forcibly tried to get the whale off the sand and into the water. They couldn't do it, so the rescuers had to make a choice.

They could walk away and let the whale die, or they could get a crane to move the whale back into the water.

The choice was easy. The details about getting the crane were worked out. What was important was that the rescuers could not let the whale die. Then, too, they did not want to disappoint the worried people who were watching. The rescuers' job, after all, was saving whales.

Quickly the killer whale got a name—Ben. Rescuers checked Ben's heart and breathing constantly. They began to stroke him and pour seawater over him. Since it was fall, this was cold work. It was also work that could not be stopped. If they stopped, Ben would die.

When night fell, the work continued. The night got colder, but the rescuers kept working. The seawater shimmered on Ben's back, keeping him alive.

Local people provided food and drinks for the rescuers. Forest rangers helped by bringing floats to help move the whale.

When the crane finally arrived, the rescuers had to wait for high tide. They wanted to make sure Ben was as near as he could be to deeper water.

When the tide was high, the rescuers put a sling around Ben. Then they attached the sling to the crane. The crane lifted the sling with the whale into the air. Then it moved over the surf.

The crane placed the whale into the ocean. Then rescuers attached the sling to a boat that towed Ben out to sea.

When the whale was safely in deep water, the boat let the sling go. The whale drifted out and then quickly swam away. Everyone on the beach cheered.

After a while, the rescuers saw the young whale playing with a larger whale. That whale, the rescuers thought, was believed to be Ben's mother. The rescuers said they seemed happy to be together.

Before the release, Ingrid Visser identified Ben so she could continue to watch for him in the ocean. She has seen Ben swimming in a pod several times since his rescue in 1997.